My Name is Lilly

A Collection of Stories about People who Share my Name

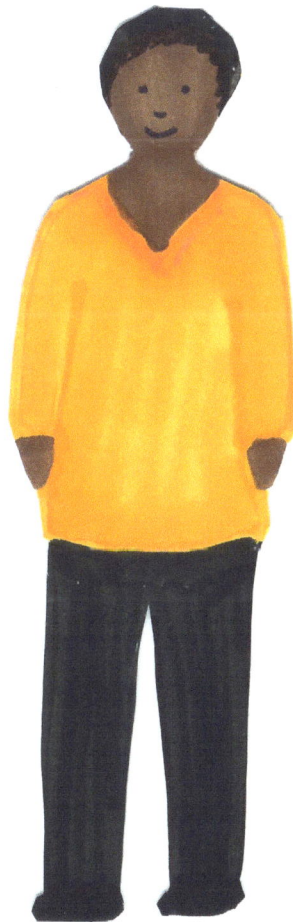

By Allison Dearstyne

For every girl named Lilly. May you always be as lovely and sweet as the flower for which you were named!

You probably already know that you share your name with a flower! Your name comes from the Latin word for the lily flower, called "lilium." In English, "lilium" is translated "Lily." A lily is a symbol of purity and innocence. In 1794, the English poet William Blake wrote a poem called "The Lilly" about true love. This is the poem:

The modest Rose puts forth a thorn,
The humble Sheep, a threatening horn:
While the Lilly white, shall in Love delight,
Nor a thorn nor a threat stain her beauty bright

We will look at the stories of seven heroes who share your name:

Lilly Ledbetter
Lily Nie
Lily Golden
Lily Yeh
Lillie Carroll Jackson
Lily Maxwell
Lillie Anna James

Lilly Ledbetter was an American hero who took an unfair situation at work and turned it into something wonderful! She was born in Alabama in 1938 in a house with no running water or electricity. She worked hard growing up, married right after she graduated from high school, then had two children.

Her children were still young when she decided to apply for her dream job at a Goodyear Tire factory. Lilly Ledbetter wanted a job as a manager, even though the only women she had seen working at Goodyear were secretaries. Against the odds, she got the position she wanted. After a few years, she was promoted to the position of area manager. But every day at work, she faced discrimination because she was a woman. People didn't think she was as qualified as men to do the job she did. Still, she was hopeful that someday at work, things would change.

And one day, things changed - just not in the way she expected. She had worked 19 years for Goodyear when she received a note from someone who kept their identity secret. The note told her that she was making thousands of dollars less every year than men in her position. Salaries are typically kept secret in private companies, so she had no idea how much Goodyear had been underpaying her for her entire career. She earned $500 less every month than the lowest paid male area manager. It wasn't fair!

So, Lilly Ledbetter decided to retire in 1998 and then sue Goodyear for discrimination. When she took them to court for treating her unfairly, she lost so she brought her case to the Supreme Court. The United States Supreme Court is the nation's highest court where cases are heard by nine Justices. Decisions made there are important because they determine the outcome of any other similar cases that come up later. To win a victory in the Supreme Court would mean victory for people in situations like Lilly Ledbetter's throughout the United States.

But the Justices did not rule in favor of Lilly Ledbetter. They told her it was too late to file a lawsuit since she didn't file right when the discrimination began. When she told the Justices that she had only just found out about being underpaid, they told her that it didn't matter. When the situation seemed hopeless, someone inspired her to keep going. After the decision was read, Justice Ruth Bader Ginsburg read her own opinion, which disagreed with the majority. She urged Lilly Ledbetter to fight back, even though she had lost twice.

As she worked to bring public attention to her case, Lilly Ledbetter said, "This cause, which bears my name, is bigger than me. It's as big as all of you. This fight, which began as my own, is now our fight—a fight for the fundamental American values that make our country great."

More lawmakers heard about her case, and they sided with her. Then in 2009, Congress passed the Lilly Ledbetter Fair Pay Act to reverse the Supreme Court's decision. It was the first law that President Barack Obama signed. After her hard-earned victory, Lilly Ledbetter traveled around the United States urging ethnic minorities and women to claim their civil rights.

Because of Lilly Ledbetter, now it is much easier for workers to receive equal pay if their company has discriminated against them. One day you will join the work force too. When you do, be thankful for heroes like Lilly Ledbetter, who helped make your paycheck fair for all the hard work you will do!

Lily Nie is the Chinese American founder of an adoption agency that has brought over 10,000 children and parents together. She was born in Yingkou, China in 1963. During her childhood and teenage years, China had a very quickly growing population which caused their government to make a strict rule for families. They were only allowed to have one child. Sadly, like so many places around the world, in China boys were valued more than girls. Because of this, a lot of parents gave their baby girls to orphanages and hoped to have a baby boy later.

When Lily Nie grew up she graduated from Fushun University with a law degree. Then she moved to the United States in 1987 to marry Joshua Zhong, and they lived in Colorado. She became the mother of twins, who filled her heart with joy and her head with thoughts of China with all of its orphans. The orphanages there were overcrowded and lacked money to support all of the children. She wondered if someday she might be able to help them.

Five years after Lily Nie moved to the United States, the laws in China changed to allow people from other countries to adopt Chinese children. Lily Nie saw this as an opportunity to help the orphans by connecting them to loving families! So she and her husband founded an organization called Chinese Children Adoption International. Together they worked with very limited resources to get a strict Chinese government to allow Americans into the country to adopt children.

Two years later, she visited the Chinese orphanages with the first American families to bring home their baby girls. Lily Nie was thrilled to see the babies adopted, but she was sad to see the distressing conditions of the orphanages. Babies were underfed, rarely held and didn't have their diapers regularly changed. Lily Nie knew she couldn't place all of the orphans in homes so she expanded her work and created a program to help the children left in orphanages.

In 1995 Lily Nie founded the Children's Charity Fund to raise money for the orphans. More staff were hired to care for the children and Chinese families were trained for foster care. The orphans' heath improved right away thanks to Lily Nie's program. Today in China's orphanages, babies are nurtured and well fed. The Chinese government did away with the one child per family law too. Things are much better now!

In 1996, Lily Nie realized that Chinese children growing up in the United States should keep a cultural connection. She expanded her work again, and opened a place in Colorado called the Joyous Chinese Cultural Center. There, adopted children connect with each other and learn about their Chinese history and customs. Later Lily Nie grew the program to lead family trips to China. Across the United States, other adoption agencies have copied her wonderful idea of cultural education.

Lily Nie and her husband adopted a special needs baby girl from China through their own program and she has thrived growing up in their family. Every year on Mother's Day, Lily Nie receives hundreds of cards of gratitude written by her own children, and the families she has helped. Because of her enormous impact on the world, Lily Nie was inducted into the Colorado Women's Hall of Fame in 2008.

Lily Nie's heart went out to children in need. She found so many ways to help them. As you grow, you will find that there are always people who need our help. Show kindness to these people and you can be like compassionate Lily Nie!

Lily Golden was a Black Russian whose mixed ancestry motivated her to fight against racial injustice. She was born in Uzbekistan in 1934, the daughter of a Black American/American Indian father and a Jewish/Polish American mother.

Lily Golden's ancestry was complex. When her parents married, they were criticized by American society for being an interracial couple so they moved to Uzbekistan where they hoped for a better life. There, her parents still faced discrimination as they adapted to life in a new country.

As Lily Golden grew, so did tension between the United States and the Soviet Union. This conflict that lasted over four decades is known as the Cold War. Uzbekistan was part of the Soviet Union, and they considered Americans to be their enemies. To hide her origins, Lily Golden was called Liya since it sounded less American.

Lily Golden moved to Russia and graduated from Moscow State University. After that she wrote books and taught classes about ethnic minorities in Russia and the Soviet Union. The role that Russian ethnic minorities played in history was often downplayed, and she brought their stories to the light.

As a scholar, Lily Golden became a hero to people in the Soviet Union. But in the United States, some people in the government viewed Lily Golden as a threat. Sometimes American newspapers published bogus stories about how much damage she was doing, beginning revolutions abroad and giving military advice to Soviet leaders. None of it was true, of course.

Lily Golden married and had one daughter. Sadly, her husband died young, so she raised their daughter alone. After her daughter grew up, Lily Golden moved to the United States, wanting to learn more about her ancestry. She was happy to meet her relatives who told her about her family history. In the United States, she used her unique heritage to represent several charities and organizations at United Nations meetings. The United Nations is an international organization whose goal is to achieve peace and cooperation worldwide. Her work there helped change the world!

Lily Golden teaches us that diversity is a great strength to any nation. Her point of view in history is one that is rarely told. Remember that all perspectives are valuable and you can be like Lily Golden!

Lily Yeh is a Chinese American artist whose projects have helped people all around the world. She was born in 1941 in Guizhou, China. She grew up in Taiwan, then moved to the the United States to attend the University of Pennsylvania Graduate School of Fine Arts. In Philadelphia Lily Yeh worked as a professor for 30 years while taking on side projects that changed the world, one community at a time.

In 1989, she became a change-leader in a rundown neighborhood in her own city. Crime rates were high, buildings were in shambles and a lot of people living there felt that things would not improve. Lily Yeh began her volunteer project by collecting trash, and meeting the curious local children and their parents. They became her teammates cleaning up the area, then planting gardens and painting wall-sized art.

The whole neighborhood became alive with hope and Lily Yeh became unstoppable! She co-founded a non-profit organization in Philadelphia called The Village of Arts and Humanities. Through this organization, she led efforts to transform 120 vacant lots into gardens and parks. Lily Yeh helped people imagine and recreate their city!

Seeing the great success of her organization in her city, she turned her attention to needy areas around the world. She led similar projects in Ghana, Rwanda, Kenya, Ecuador, China, and Germany. Some of the people Lily Yeh worked with had lived through great tragedies. She helped them to envision and build memorials. Some of the people Lily Yeh worked with were in danger of losing their cultural identity from decades under harsh government rule. Lily Yeh listened to their stories, and together they created art which brought their cultural heritage back to their villages.

During her time doing projects worldwide, Lily Yeh founded another non-profit organization called Barefoot Artists Inc. She trained local people, organized communities and used art to transform spaces, this time on a global scale. Both of the organizations she founded are still running today!

She said, "I have found that the broken spaces are my living canvas. In our brokenness, our hearts reach for beauty." We learn from Lily Yeh that we each have something valuable to offer. So contribute like Lily Yeh, because you are important!

Lillie Carroll Jackson was a Black American Civil Rights leader known as the "Mother of Freedom." In 1889 she was born in Baltimore, Maryland. At that time, Black Americans did not have the same rights as White Americans. As she grew, Lillie Carroll Jackson became determined to change that. Life in the church was always a big part of her life. She was the daughter of a minister and she married a minister. Together they had four children.

Before she was 30, she faced a huge crisis. She had an infection inside of her head that decayed her bones so much that she was not expected to live very long. She prayed and asked God to spare her life so that she could raise her children. Surgery saved her life, but it permanently disfigured her face. Thankful to have survived such trauma, she dedicated her life to serving God.

Lillie Carroll Jackson raised her children to believe that they had great value. When they grew up, they all fought for equal rights for Black Americans. One method they used was boycotting. A boycott is when a lot of people punish a business by refusing to shop there. In 1931, Lillie Carroll Jackson and her daughter Juanita created a campaign in Baltimore called "Buy Where You Can Work." The idea was that if a workplace would not hire Black people, their business would lose customers and money.

The boycott worked! In other cities across the country, people copied their good idea. Decades later, Martin Luther King, Jr. used her strategy of nonviolent resistance to bring about change. For this reason she was called the "Mother of the Civil Rights Movement." She was also called "Ma Jackson" by the many people who loved her.

She joined forces with the NAACP, or National Association for the Advancement of Colored People. The NAACP was, and still is, an organization with the goal of helping Black Americans achieve equal treatment. For 35 years, she served as president for the Baltimore branch. During those years, she made great strides toward achieving equality.

You will learn more about the Civil Rights Movement in school as you get older. When you do, think about strong Lillie Carroll Jackson, who didn't let anything stop her from fighting for what was right.

Lily Maxwell was the first British woman to vote in an election long before it was legal for women to vote! She was born to a poor family in Scotland around 1800 and grew up in Manchester. For several decades she worked as a servant for a wealthy businessman. Over the years, she saved money and learned enough about running a business to open her own shop.

As a shopkeeper, she paid local taxes. In 1867, there was an election for a Member of Parliament, which is part of the government in Britain. All men who paid shopkeeper taxes were allowed to vote, and by mistake Lily Maxwell's name appeared on a list of registered voters. Somebody had messed up by including her name because women weren't allowed to vote.

Word got around about this mistake to a suffragist named Lydia Becker. A suffragist is someone who wants equal voting rights for everyone. Lydia Becker encouraged Lily Maxwell to vote. Back then in Britain, people voted by going to their local polling station and loudly announcing their choice of candidate.

The two women went together to the polling station, and Lily Maxwell confidently announced her choice for a candidate, a suffragist named Jacob Bright. Since Lily Maxwell was listed as a registered voter, the officers had to accept her vote. Although plenty of men at the polling station didn't like this, she had enough supporters in the room to make it explode in cheers for the first woman to vote!

Lydia Becker used Lily Maxwell's example to create a case that went to court. Over 5,000 career-women requested the right to vote because they earned income and paid taxes. But unfortunately, they lost their case in court. After that, it took 50 years for women to win the right to vote in Britain.

Voting is such an important right that we have today because of the hard work of so many people who went before us. One day when you vote, think about courageous Lily Maxwell!

Lillie Anna "Mother" James was a Black American educator who established a school for Black children. She was born in 1876 in Pensacola, Florida, where she lived her entire life.

You remember from Lillie Carroll Jackson's story how Black Americans did not have the same rights as White Americans, which made life hard for them. For Lillie Anna James, life was especially difficult because she grew up in the Deep South. Slavery had only recently become illegal when she was born and Black people struggled to make a living. A passion grew within her to help.

She married Daniel James in 1894 and together they had 17 children! Lillie Anna James opened a private school for her own children and other Black children who were not allowed to attend the White schools. It was called the "Lillie A. James Private School" and she ran it with pride her whole life long. Passionate for her children to prove their worth, her 11th commandment was "Thou shalt not quit."

Lillie Anna James inspired many to greatness, including her son Daniel "Chappie" James, Jr. When he grew up he became a fighter pilot in the Air Force and instructed other pilots during War War II. He made his mother proud when he became the first Black American to become a four-star general in the United States Armed Forces.

Mothers like Lillie Anna James are not often recognized publicly for all the care they give, but raising such remarkable children was among her life's greatest achievements. Her life proves that you don't have to be famous to make a huge difference. When you are faced with a difficult task, just remember Lillie Anna James' 11th commandment, because you can do hard things!

This page is all about you!

_____ was born on

_____

As a baby, Lilly _____

_____

As a little girl, Lilly _____

_____

Lilly is especially good at _____

_____

Lilly is often described as _____

_____

Lilly makes people laugh when she _____

_____

One day Lilly would like to _____

_____

This page is for making a self-portrait. A self-portrait is a picture of you, drawn by you!

Bibliography

Artist Lily Yeh Transforms Communities Around the World. *Healing-power-of-art.org.* Web. 24 Mar. 2022

Coen, Ross. Lillie M. Carroll Jackson (1889-1975). *blackpast.org.* 13 Aug 2020. Web. 01 Jul. 2021.

Dr. Lillie May Carroll Jackson, civil rights leader. *baltimoresun.com.* 10 Feb. 2007. Web. 01 Jul. 2021.

Ernst, Alina. "Lily Golden (1934-2010)." *blackpast.org.* 07 Jul. 2018. Web. 03 Apr. 2022

"Lily Golden, the Russian African-American social activist, has died." Afro-Europe International Blog. *afroeurope.blogspot.com* 18 Feb. 2011. Web. 03 Apr. 2022

"Lilly Ledbetter." *lillyledbetter.com.* Web. 10 Jun. 2021.

"Lily Maxwell: The first woman to vote." The History Press. *Thehistorypress.co.uk.* Web. 28 Feb. 2022.

"Lily Nie." Colorado Women's Hall of Fame. *cogreatwomen.org.* Web. 30 Mar. 2021.

"Lily Yeh." *pps.org.* 31 Dec. 2008. Web. 24 Mar 2022.

Martin, Claire. "Couple's efforts transform system, find homes for thousands of Chinese orphans." The Denver Post. *denverpost.com* 04 May 2016. Web. 13 May 2021.

Pompilio, Natalie. "Lily Yeh. Beauty in Broken Places." *yesmagazine.org.* 20 Dec. 2011. Web 13 May 2021.

Wikipedia contributors. "Lillie Mae Carroll Jackson." *Wikipedia, The Free Encyclopedia. Wikipedia, The Free Encyclopedia*, 4 Jun. 2021. Web. 2 Jul. 2021.

Wikipedia contributors. "Lillie Anna James." *Wikipedia, The Free Encyclopedia. Wikipedia,* The Free Encyclopedia, 3 Oct. 2021. Web. 2 Apr. 2022.

Wikipedia contributors. "Lilly Ledbetter." *Wikipedia, The Free Encyclopedia. Wikipedia,* The Free Encyclopedia, 10 May. 2021. Web. 11 Jun. 2021.

Wikipedia contributors. "Lily Nie." *Wikipedia, The Free Encyclopedia. Wikipedia, The Free Encyclopedia*, 31 Mar. 2020. Web. 11 May. 2021.

Wikipedia contributors. "Lily Yeh." *Wikipedia, The Free Encyclopedia. Wikipedia, The Free Encyclopedia,* 26 Dec. 2021. Web. 25 Mar. 2022.

Wikipedia contributors. "The Lilly (poem)." *Wikipedia, The Free Encyclopedia. Wikipedia, The Free Encyclopedia,* 1 Jun. 2021. Web. 10 Jun. 2021.